JUN 2010

GLOBALHOTSPOTS

NORTH KOREA

Clive Gifford

mc Marshall Cavendish
Benchmark
New York

This edition first published in 2010 in the United States of America by
MARSHALL CAVENDISH BENCHMARK
An imprint of Marshall Cavendish Corporation

Website: www.marshallcavendish.us

This publication represents the opinions and views of the author based on Clive Gifford's personal experience,
knowledge, and research. The information in this book serves as a general guide only. The author and publisher
have used their best efforts in preparing this book and disclaim liability rising directly and indirectly from the use
and application of this book.

Other Marshall Cavendish Offices:
Marshall Cavendish Ltd. 5th Floor, 32-38 Saffron Hill, London EC1N 8 FH, UK • Marshall Cavendish International
(Asia) Private Limited, 1 New Industrial Road, Singapore 536196 • Marshall Cavendish International (Thailand)
Co Ltd. 253 Asoke, 12th Flr, Sukhumvit 21 Road, Klongtoey Nua, Wattana, Bangkok 10110, Thailand • Marshall
Cavendish (Malaysia) Sdn Bhd, Times Subang, Lot 46, Subang Hi-Tech Industrial Park, Batu Tiga, 40000 Shah Alam,
Selangor Darul Ehsan, Malaysia

Marshall Cavendish is a trademark of Times Publishing Limited

All websites were available and accurate when this book was sent to press.

Library of Congress Cataloging-in-Publication Data

Gifford, Clive.
    North Korea / Clive Gifford.
      p. cm. — (Global hotspots)
    Includes index.
    Summary: "Discusses North Korea, its history, conflicts, and the reasons why it is currently in the news"—
    Provided by publisher.
    ISBN 978-0-7614-4761-0
    1. Korea (North)—Juvenile literature. I. Title.
    DS932.G53 2011
951.93—dc22

                                        2009039779

First published in 2010 by
MACMILLAN EDUCATION AUSTRALIA PTY LTD
15–19 Claremont Street, South Yarra 3141

Visit our website at www.macmillan.com.au or go directly to www.macmillanlibrary.com.au

Associated companies and representatives throughout the world.

 Produced for Macmillan Education Australia by
MONKEY PUZZLE MEDIA LTD
48 York Avenue, Hove BN3 1PJ, UK

Edited by Susie Brooks
Text and cover design by Tom Morris and James Winrow
Page layout by Tom Morris
Photo research by Susie Brooks and Lynda Lines
Maps by Martin Darlison, Encompass Graphics

Printed in the United States

Acknowledgments
The author and the publisher are grateful to the following for permission to reproduce copyright material:

Front cover photograph: North Korean soldiers stand guard at the Demilitarised Zone that divides North and South Korea.
Courtesy of Corbis (Michel Setboun).

Corbis, **12** (Bettmann), **13** (Bettmann), **18** (Alain Le Garsmeur), **23** (Korea Pool/Yonhap/epa), **29** (Reuters); Getty Images,
4 (AFP), **6** (Ed Fremman), **7** (Hulton Archive), **8** (Hulton Archive), **9** (Time & Life Pictures), **10**, **11** (Time & Life Pictures),
14 (AFP), **15** (Time & Life Pictures), **17** (AFP), **19** (Time & Life Pictures), **20**, **21** (David Hume Kennerly), **22** (AFP), **24**, **25** (AFP),
26, **27** (AFP), **28** (AFP); iStockphoto, **30**.

While every care has been taken to trace and acknowledge copyright, the publisher tenders their apologies for any
accidental infringement where copyright has proved untraceable. Where the attempt has been unsuccessful, the
publisher welcomes information that would redress the situation.

1 3 5 6 4 2

CONTENTS

Glossary Words

When a word is printed in **bold**, you can look
up its meaning in the Glossary on page 31.

ALWAYS IN THE NEWS

Global hot spots are places that are always in the news. They are places where there has been conflict between different groups of people for years. Sometimes the conflicts have lasted for hundreds of years.

Why Do Hot Spots Happen?

There are four main reasons why hot spots happen:

1 Disputes over land, and who has the right to live on it.

2 Disagreements over religion and **culture**, where different peoples find it impossible to live happily side-by-side.

3 Arguments over how the government should be organized.

4 Conflict over resources, such as oil, gold, or diamonds.

Sometimes these disagreements spill over into violence—and into the headlines.

MASSIVE MILITARY

STATISTICS

North Korea is believed to have the fifth-largest army in the world, with more than 1.2 million members. One in five of all Korean men age 17 to 54 are active soldiers. At least 4 million more are reserves.

North Korean soldiers march in the capital city of Pyongyang. They carry a banner showing Kim Jong-Il, their country's leader.

North Korea as a Hot Spot

North Korea has been a hot spot since it was split from South Korea in 1948. The two countries had been one nation for hundreds of years. After a bitter **civil war** in the 1950s, the two countries are still close to conflict today.

A Secretive Country

The North Korean government is very secretive. It discourages visitors, and information about the country is scarce. Because of this secrecy, many other nations are concerned about North Korea's plans. They are especially worried because it has tested nuclear weapons. Between 2002 and 2008, the United States placed North Korea on a list of nations it believes **sponsor** terrorism.

"It raises a serious threat to peace, not only for the Korean peninsula, but for the region."

Former South Korean President, Roh Moo Hyun, in response to North Korea's nuclear testing.

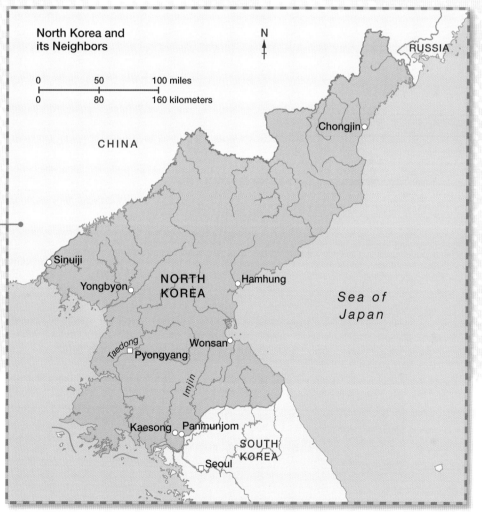

North Korea shares a short land border with Russia, and longer borders with China and South Korea.

A CLOSED NATION

For hundreds of years, before being split into North and South, Korea was a "closed" country. It did not allow foreign influences, and protected its borders fiercely.

The Joseon Dynasty

The Joseon dynasty, sometimes called the New Chosŏn dynasty, ruled Korea from 1392 to 1910. During that time, Korea had very little contact with the rest of the world. It tended to trade only with China, on Korea's northern border.

Religion

Koreans were traditionally followers of the **Confucian** religion. From the 1780s onward, **missionaries** began introducing Christianity to Korea. The *Taewŏn'gun* (meaning Grand Prince) reacted by outlawing Christianity in 1864. Several French missionaries were killed.

Gyeongbok Palace, in the city of Seoul, was built more than 600 years ago when the Joseon dynasty of emperors ran Korea.

Attempts to Trade with Korea

In the late 1800s, the outside world tried to form trading links with Korea. France and the United States, in particular, wanted to **exploit** the country's resources, such as coal. But Korea felt that it had nothing to gain or learn from other countries, and resisted any attempts to trade with outsiders.

HOT SPOT BRIEFING

FIRST CLASH
The first-ever clash between Korea and a Western power occurred in 1866. French forces invaded Ganghwa Island, off Korea's west coast. However, they failed to advance far and decided to leave before the harsh winter arrived.

"The expedition I just accomplished, however modest as it is, may have prepared the ground for a more serious one if deemed necessary... The expedition deeply shocked the Korean Nation."

Admiral Pierre-Gustave Roze, leader of the 1866 French expedition.

In 1871, five U.S. ships tried to build friendly relations with Korea. Instead, a battle broke out and 300 Koreans were killed. The Americans captured this Korean flag.

THE THREAT FROM JAPAN

By the early 1900s, Japan had become the strongest country in the Far East. Japan was an ancient rival of Korea's, and was determined to expand its power throughout the region.

Japan Invades

In 1910, Japanese forces invaded Korea. Inside Korea, Japanese **assassins** had paved the way by killing the Korean Empress Myseongseong in 1895. The Empress had been in favor of fewer ties with Japan, and closer links with Russia. Now that she was gone, Japan faced less opposition.

Exploiting Korea

After invading, the Japanese quickly began to exploit Korea. Japanese farmers seized a lot of Korean farmland. Tens of thousands of pieces of Korean art were stolen. Korean people were forced to work as little more than slaves. For millions of Koreans, life under the Japanese became very tough.

Japanese policemen keep a crowd quiet in Korea. Japan's soldiers and police often used brutal tactics when Korea was under their control.

Rebel Groups

Rebel groups soon sprang up to fight the Japanese and try to force them out of Korea. Among the rebels were members of the **Communist** Party of Korea, which had formed in secret in 1925. Many communist rebels moved into China, but crossed the border to perform hit-and-run attacks on the Japanese.

FORCED LABOR DURING WWII

During World War II, Japan forced many Koreans to work in mines and factories in appalling conditions.
- Around 5,400,000 Koreans became forced laborers.
- Of these, 640,000 of these were taken to work in Japan.
- Up to 810,000 forced laborers died.

These Korean laborers, some children, were forced to work for the Japanese during World War II.

DIVIDED IN TWO

The Japanese were forced to leave Korea in 1945, after the end of World War II. Koreans rejoiced, but it would not be long before their country was divided.

The U.S. and USSR

After World War II, the United States and the **USSR** both wanted to control Korea. They would not work together, so the world's two most powerful countries agreed to split Korea in two. The USSR controlled the north, and the United States controlled the south. The arrangement was meant to last only until all the Japanese troops in Korea had surrendered and left.

"The three great powers [China, the U.S. and the U.K.], mindful of the enslavement of the people of Korea, are determined that in due course Korea shall become free and independent."

The Cairo Declaration, 1943—a statement made after a meeting of the leaders of China, the United States, and the United Kingdom.

Students welcome United States forces into Korea in 1945. Japanese control of Korea was over, but the country would shortly be split in two.

Temporary Governments

Both the United States and the USSR set up temporary governments that reflected their own political views. In the south, the United States appointed an anti-communist leader called Syngman Rhee. In the north, the USSR installed a communist leader, Kim Song-Il.

Permanent Division

Eventually, the two "temporary" Korean governments became permanent. This happened because the United States and USSR could not agree on how to reunite Korea. **Soviet** troops left North Korea in 1948, but the two governments still became more and more **hostile** toward each other.

American soldiers man a roadblock on the 38th Parallel. This line on the map divided Korea in two halves, one controlled by the United States, the other by the USSR.

THE KOREAN WAR: 1950–1953

The Korean War began in June 1950. It started when North Korean troops crossed the 38th Parallel and invaded South Korea.

UN Troops

The **United Nations** (UN) agreed to send a large force of troops to stop North Korea from waging war on the South. Sixteen nations sent soldiers. The United States sent the largest number by far. The UN troops in Korea were led by an American, General Douglas MacArthur.

"My mission was to clear out all North Korea, to unify it and to liberalize it."

General Douglas MacArthur, talking to the United States Congress in May 1951, a month after President Truman removed him from command of forces in Korea.

Douglas MacArthur (pictured here) clashed with U.S. President Truman over the Korean War. MacArthur wanted to attack Chinese bases, but Truman feared this would anger the USSR and bring them into the war.

China Joins In

China sent tens of thousands of troops to support North Korea. This occurred after the UN forces had driven the North Korean invaders back inside their own country. Chinese reinforcements allowed North Korea to invade South Korea again, at the end of 1950.

No Clear Winner

From the middle of 1951 onward, neither side made great advances. The war continued to be fought roughly along the 38th Parallel. Peace talks lasted for more than two years before an **armistice** agreement was signed in July 1953.

KOREAN WAR DEATHS

STATISTICS

North Koreans	500,000
South Koreans	1,300,000
Chinese	1,000,000
Americans	37,000
Other UN members	3,350

The USS *Missouri* was the first American battleship to reach Korean waters during the war. Its heavy guns were used to pound North Korean forces on the coast.

THE GREAT LEADER

The end of the war left North Korea devastated and with almost the same territory that it had when it started. But its self-styled "Great Leader," Kim Song-Il (also spelled Kim Sung-Il) held on to power.

Strengthening His Grip

Kim Song-Il acted quickly to increase his grip on government. He blamed rivals for failures during the war and had them removed from power. Many were held in giant prison camps or **executed**. In their place, he appointed people who were loyal to him.

HOT SPOT BRIEFING

CULT FOLLOWING
Kim built up a cult-like following in North Korea. He was called the "Great Leader," and there were frequent parades honoring him. His image was found throughout North Korea and more than 800 statues of him were built.

This statue of Kim Song-Il was built in 1972 to celebrate his 60th birthday. It is one of hundreds of likenesses of Kim found throughout North Korea.

Repairing the Damage

North Korea's capital city, Pyongyang, was flattened by bombing during the Korean War. It was rebuilt with aid from China and the USSR. Further aid allowed North Korea to recover its steel industry, and other industries.

Controlling Information

Kim allowed in little information from the outside world. North Koreans were not allowed to travel overseas and Kim made sure that the media was strictly controlled. As a result, many young North Koreans grew up believing their government's view of the world.

"I didn't know about America, or China or the fact that the Korean **Peninsula** was divided and there was a place called South Korea."

Teenager Shin Dong Hyok, who was born in a North Korean prison camp.

North Korea's towns and cities were devastated by the war. Thousands of buildings, bridges, roads, and dams needed to be rebuilt, at a high price.

THE DEMILITARIZED ZONE

The 1953 armistice agreement created a **Demilitarized Zone (or DMZ for short)** between North and South Korea. Both sides have positioned thousands of troops along their edge of the DMZ.

Empty Land

The DMZ is an empty strip of land, 2.5 miles (4 kilometers) wide, which separates North and South Korea. Running down the middle of the DMZ is the Military Demarcation Line. Neither side is allowed to cross this line, although troops sometimes enter the side of the DMZ nearest to them.

HOT SPOT BRIEFING

ASSASSINATION ATTEMPT
In 1968, 31 North Korean **commandos** tried to assassinate the South Korean president, Park Chung Hee. They secretly crossed the DMZ disguised as South Korean soldiers. Their attempt was unsuccessful and 30 of the commandos died.

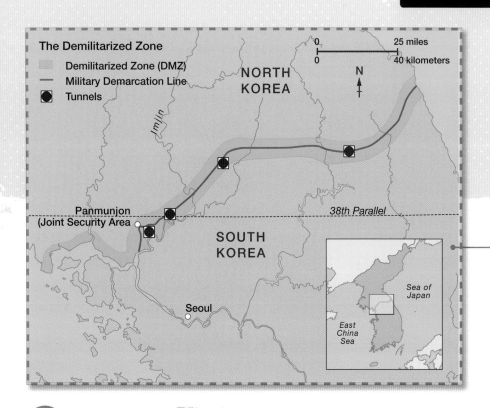

The Demilitarized Zone

- Demilitarized Zone (DMZ)
- Military Demarcation Line
- Tunnels

NORTH KOREA

Imjin

Panmunjon (Joint Security Area)

38th Parallel

SOUTH KOREA

Seoul

Sea of Japan

East China Sea

The Demilitarised Zone crosses the 38th Parallel at an angle. It is the most heavily armed border in the world.

The Joint Security Area

The Joint Security Area is the one place in the middle of the DMZ where North and South Korea meet. It is close to where the armistice was signed in 1953. Officials from both Koreas have met here to hold talks.

Trouble in the DMZ

Tension between the opposing forces has led to many moments of trouble. Raids crossing the DMZ have occurred, and North Korean tunnels under the DMZ have been discovered. More than 600 people have died in exchanges of gunfire across the DMZ since it was established.

HOT SPOT BRIEFING

AMERICAN DEATHS
In 1976, two U.S. servicemen were killed and four injured by North Korean soldiers. They had entered the Joint Security Area to trim tree branches blocking the view of their observation points.

North Korean border guards march close to the Joint Security Area. North Korea often displays large numbers of soldiers at the border in shows of strength.

THAWING RELATIONS?

North and South Korea tried to negotiate peacefully during the 1970s and 1980s. But many of these attempts were stopped due to hostile actions from one side or the other.

The First Talks

The first major peace talks between the North and South, since the Korean War, began at the Joint Security Area in 1971. The following year the two nations agreed that if North and South Korea were ever to become one nation, it should be done peacefully and without foreign influences. However, both sides had different views on how the peace talks should progress. They were unable to agree, and the talks halted suddenly in 1973.

HOT SPOT BRIEFING

KIDNAPPING OPPONENTS
In August 1973, South Korea's opposition leader, Kim Dae-Jung, was kidnapped by the South Korean spy agency, the KCIA. Kim was a supporter of unifying the two Koreas. North Korea walked out of talks as a result.

North and South Korean negotiators sit down for talks. The two countries have met on a number of occasions, but little lasting agreement has occurred.

1980s – Talks Stall

The 1980s saw little real progress. There were periods of improved relations, but these were mixed with skirmishes along the DMZ, as well as incidents of terrorism and spying. North Koreans, for example, attempted to assassinate the South Korean leader, President Chun Doo Hwan, whilst he visited Burma (Myanmar). A year later, however, the North Korean government sent aid to the victims of floods in South Korea.

South Korean opposition leader, Kim Dae-Jung, waves to a large crowd in 1989. He and many of his supporters were in favor of continuing talks with North Korea.

SELF-RELIANCE?

North Korea built up its economy so that it did not have to trade much with others. This was part of Kim Song-Il's policy of *Juche*, meaning self-reliance. After a strong start, the country struggled to meet its citizens' needs.

Changes to the Economy

North Korea's economy went through major changes in the 1950s and 1960s. Farmers were forced to work together on giant, **communal** farms. Industries were built up, and the country's economy grew at a rapid rate, often by 30 percent per year.

Struggling Yet Spending

After 20 years of good times, North Korea's economy struggled in the 1970s. This was for many reasons, including a reduction in aid from China and the USSR. Yet, despite its problems, the country continued to spend heavily on the military.

The 558-feet (170-meter) tall Juche Tower commemorates Kim Song-Il's policy of self-reliance. The three figures show a factory worker, a farmer and a working writer.

A Growing Population

Between 1953 and 2000, North Korea's population almost tripled in size. Farms struggled to meet the increasing demand for food. The country's industries could not sell enough goods overseas to cover the cost of importing food. Shortages of food and other basic goods occurred frequently.

North Korean children, suffering from hunger, lie on the floor of an orphanage. Thousands of North Koreans suffered from disease and lack of food during the 1990s.

"North Korea does not grow enough food to feed its population ... it's a mountainous country, and it may not be food **self-sufficient** ever."

Catherine Bertini, World Food Programme executive director, talking about food aid given to North Korea in 2001.

A NEW LEADER

Kim Song-Il died in 1994 and his eldest son, Kim Jong-Il, came to power. He had been groomed for leadership by his father since the 1970s. He remains in power today.

A Military Man

Kim Jong-Il had become supreme commander of the North Korean armed forces in 1991. In 1995, as North Korea's leader, he began a policy called Military First to keep the forces on his side. This policy put even more money into the military, at a time when many North Koreans were starving.

MILITARY SPENDING

STATISTICS

Military spending is sometimes shown as a percentage of the total Gross Domestic Product (GDP) of a nation. This list compares North Korea's military spending with other countries.

North Korea	22.9%
China	4.3%
United States	4.1%
Russia	3.9%
South Korea	2.7%
United Kingdom	2.4%

An enormous military parade is held in Pyongyang in 2007. It consists of thousands of serving soldiers and a number of mobile missile launchers.

Mysterious Leader

The outside world knows relatively little about Kim Jong-Il. He receives few foreign guests and rarely makes trips to other countries. When visiting Moscow in 2001, he took a 6,214-mile (10,000-kilometer) train journey from Pyongyang, because it is believed that he fears flying.

Reforms But Little Difference

Kim Jong-Il has made some **reforms** and allowed some foreign investment in North Korea. But the country is still run as a secret state, and its people remain desperately poor.

"He's crazy like a fox, he's unpredictable, he's reckless but you have to take him seriously."

Bill Richardson, former U.S. ambassador to the United Nations, talking about Kim Jong-Il.

In 2000, Kim Jong-Il (on the right) met with South Korean President Kim Dae-Jung. It was the first time a South Korean leader had traveled to North Korea. Dae-Jung won the Nobel Peace Prize as a result.

NUCLEAR WEAPONS

A crisis developed in the 1990s when North Korea appeared to be working toward building nuclear weapons. The country had asked for nuclear weapons in the 1950s, but the USSR had refused.

Weapons from Power Stations

Some types of nuclear power station can produce the radioactive material needed to make nuclear weapons. By the 1990s, North Korea had built its own nuclear power stations, including one at Yongbyon. This sparked growing international fears that North Korea was developing its own nuclear weapons.

U.S. v North Korea

The United States and North Korea clashed many times on the nuclear issue. The two countries made an agreement in 1994 that the United States would donate massive fuel aid if North Korea stopped researching nuclear weapons. But suspicions remained that North Korea accepted the fuel aid and continued its weapons work in secret.

This U.S. satellite photograph shows the Yongbyon nuclear plant in North Korea.

Six Party Talks

Six Party Talks began in 2003. These were meetings between six nations: China, Russia, Japan, the United States, and North and South Korea. The other nations wanted North Korea to halt its nuclear research, but North Korea insisted it was developing nuclear power for peaceful purposes.

"Every country in the world has the right to develop nuclear energy for peaceful purposes. Why does the United States insist that only we should give up that right?"

The government-run North Korean newspaper, *Rodong Sinmun*, in 2005.

The leading negotiators of (from left to right) the United States, South Korea, China, North Korea, Japan, and Russia gather for the 2004 Six Party Talks.

EXPLOSIVE EVENTS

In October 2006, North Korea announced that it had successfully tested a nuclear weapon. This announcement shocked the world.

The World Reacts

The reaction around the world to North Korea's news was negative. Even countries that were usually friendly toward North Korea, such as Russia and China, condemned the act. Most world leaders feared it would lead to other countries in the region trying to gain nuclear weapons.

"Russia definitely condemns the test in North Korea."

Russian President, Vladimir Putin.

South Korean protesters take part in an anti-nuclear demonstration in Seoul.

체르노빌을 기억하라!
REMEMBER CHERNOBYL!
NO NUKE

Forcing an Agreement

Some countries tried to force North Korea to make an agreement. The United States, for example, stopped supplying large amounts of fuel aid to the country. In December 2006, these efforts were successful. The Six Party Talks restarted. In 2007, North Korea agreed to halt its nuclear program and allow inspections. In return, it would receive aid and fuel.

Changing Plans

Since 2007, work on dismantling the Yongbyon **nuclear reactor** has started and stopped several times. In October 2008, North Korea threatened to start rebuilding the reactor. To stop this, the United States agreed to remove North Korea from its list of countries that sponsor terrorism. North Korea continues to bargain hard for further benefits.

"We need to make a stern response [to North Korea's nuclear plans] and North Korea will be responsible for all the consequences."

Japanese Prime Minister, Shinzo Abe.

The cooling tower at North Korea's Yongbyon nuclear plant was demolished in June 2008, as shown on this South Korean TV program.

뉴스특보
북 냉각탑 폭파

YTN

● [미국프로야구] 추신수(클리블랜드), 샌프란시스코전에서 4타수

THE FUTURE OF NORTH KOREA

North Korea's future is uncertain. Will it become more aggressive or peaceful? Will it become increasingly isolated from other countries or work with them more? Could North and South Korea ever become one country again?

One Korea?

Unification appears unlikely in the near future. South Korea tried to improve relations for ten years with little success. In 2008, it elected a new leader with a tougher attitude toward North Korea. More and more South Koreans are now wary of unification because of the great poverty in the north.

"We don't want to achieve unification in a quick period of time because the economic costs of unification are huge."

Park Jong Chul, senior researcher at the Korea Institute of National Reunification, South Korea.

South Koreans release balloons carrying leaflets over the border into North Korea. The leaflets warn North Korean citizens about their government and leader.

Who Comes Next?

Kim Jong-Il is believed to suffer from ill health and it is unclear who will succeed him. Kim has a number of sons but they are young and inexperienced. Senior generals, instead, may decide to take power.

Instability and Hostility

Further instability in North Korea worries the world. The country remains hostile to both South Korea and South Korea's greatest ally, the United States. North Korea has a giant army a short march from South Korea and may still have the ability to rebuild its nuclear weapons.

HOT SPOT BRIEFING

SATELLITE OR MISSILE?
In April 2009, North Korea announced that it had launched a space satellite. Other nations condemned the action, believing that North Korea was really testing a long-range missile.

A boy looks at a display of missiles at the Korean War Memorial Museum. North Korea continues to make the news for its development of long-range missiles.

FIND OUT MORE

FACTFINDER
North Korea

The flag of
North Korea

Full Name Democratic People's Republic of Korea

Capital Pyongyang

Area 46,540 square miles
(120,540 square kilometers)

Population 22,665,345 (July 2009 estimate)

Rate of population change +0.42% per year

Industries Military products, machine building, electric power, chemicals, mining, metals

Gross Domestic Product* per person US$1,700
(2008 estimate)

Percentage of labor force in agriculture 37%

Number of phone lines 1.18 million

Number of TV stations 4

South Korea

The flag of
South Korea

Full Name Republic of Korea

Capital Seoul

Area 38,023 square miles
(98,480 square kilometers)

Population 48,508,972 (July 2009 estimate)

Rate of population change +0.27% per year

Industries Electronics, telecommunications, automobile production, chemicals, shipbuilding, steel

Gross Domestic Product* per person US$26,000
(2008 estimate)

Percentage of labor force in agriculture 7.2%

Number of phone lines 23.905 million

Number of TV stations 57

FOCUS QUESTIONS

These questions might help you to think about some of the issues raised in *North Korea*.

Leadership and Government

What different styles of government has North Korea had since 1900?

Economy

Is North Korea justified in spending so much of its money on the army? How has this spending affected the rest of North Korea's economy?

Politics

How has North Korea been affected by the actions of other countries? Were the United States and the USSR right to split Korea in two?

Citizenship

How are the lives of North Koreans different from the lives of South Koreans, Australians or Americans? Should North Korea allow more visitors from abroad?

* Gross Domestic Product, or GDP, is the value of all the goods and services produced by a country in a year.
(Source for statistics: *CIA World Factbook*)

GLOSSARY

armistice agreement to stop fighting in a war, usually while an attempt is made to negotiate peace

assassin someone who is instructed to kill a person, often a political figure

civil war war between different groups within their own country

commandos soldiers usually trained to perform secret missions, often in enemy territory

communal belonging to the whole community

communist based on a system where the government, rather than individual people, own farms, factories, and businesses, and these are not run to make money

Confucian based on the teachings of the Chinese philosopher, Confucius

culture skills that make a society or people distinctive, such as their language, clothes, food, music, songs, and stories

Demilitarized Zone (DMZ) area of land that large military forces are not allowed to enter

executed killed as a punishment

exploit make use of for profit, often unfairly

famine devastating shortage of food, which usually occurs when crops fail because of floods or a severe lack of rain

hostile aggressive toward or strongly opposed to

missionaries people sent on a mission, often to persuade or convert others to a particular religion or cause

nuclear reactor device that generates energy in a controlled way, mostly used to produce electricity

peninsula narrow piece of land that juts out into an area of water

reforms social or political changes

reserves people trained to be part of a military force but not actively serving

self-sufficient able to provide for one's own needs without help from others

Soviet from or of the USSR

sponsor help to fund, encourage or organize

unification joining together

United Nations organization set up after World War II that aims to help countries end disputes without fighting

USSR very powerful country that broke apart in 1991; most of it became the Russian Federation

INDEX